POEMS

گزیدۀ شعر

Azita Ghahreman

POEMS

گزیدهٔ شعر

poetry translation centre

First published in 2012
by The Poetry Translation Centre Ltd
PO Box 61051
London SE16 4YY

www.poetrytranslation.org

Poems © Azita Ghahreman, 2012

Translations from the Farsi © Maura Dooley and Elhum Shakerifar
Introduction © Elhum Shakerifar

ISBN: 978-0-9560576-8-6

The Poetry Translation Centre gratefully acknowledges the
financial support of Arts Council England.

British Library Cataloguing-in-Publication Data.
A catalogue record for this book is available from the British Library

Designed in Albertina by Libanus Press
Printed in the UK by Imprint Digital

Contents

Introduction	6
The First Rains of Spring	9
With a Red Flower	11
Glaucoma	13
Letter	17
The Boat that Brought Me	19
When Winter Comes	21
Snow	25
But	27
Happy Valentine	29

Introduction

Azita Ghahreman, born in Mashhad in 1962, is one of Iran's leading poets. She has lived and worked in Sweden since 2006, and now publishes in both languages.

Much of Azita's work is deeply personal yet is infused with political undertones. Her poems often reflect on her childhood growing up in a land-owning family in the South-Eastern Khorasan province of Iran, and on the changing face of modern Iran. In the poem 'Glaucoma', taken from her third collection of poetry, *Forgetfulness is a Simple Ritual* (1992), the changes to Iran's political landscape are referenced as gradual blindness that slowly blurs the vision. Azita depicts her own family who, despite their differing affiliations and beliefs still remain deeply connected, in the same way that Iran – a country that is home to numerous ethnicities and belief systems – continues to retain its united entity.

Thinkers and political leaders are often referenced by name: the philosopher, Nietzsche; the physicist, Oppenheimer; and Patrice Lumumba, the Congolese independence leader of the 1960s, all find their way into Azita's work. The censored and unspoken are also present: in 'When Winter Comes', the narrator warms herself at the fire created by her burning books. 'With a Red Flower', taken from the collection *Sculptures of Autumn* (1986), is dedicated to a lost friend whose name can only be read between the lines of a poem; much like the poppies one wears to remember veterans in the UK, the red flower in Iran represents political prisoners.

Azita's most recent collection *The Suburb of Crows* (2008) reflects on her exile in Sweden. 'The Boat that Brought Me' tells of the burdens of exile, the loss of one's homeland and of her first impressions of Sweden:

> Sometimes I miss
> the boat that brought me here,
> now that I am witness to the icy eyes of a Swedish winter,
> under these tired old clouds,
> while that suitcase still holds a patch of the sky-blue me.

'When Winter Comes' sees the years in exile pass quickly and quietly, 'galloping by like a wild, dark horse'.

A constant and most refreshing theme throughout Azita's work is her unusual approach to the classic theme of love. When it comes to love, the poet's grave and solemn voice becomes playful. In 'First Rains of Spring', we are advised that it is best to 'keep love at bay'; for, in the end,

> …what have we gained from it?
> Only the last winds of autumn,
> the first rains of spring.

In the poem 'Happy Valentine', published here for the first time, the poet becomes wicked and taunting as she enumerates the calamities she will bring upon her lover:

> I'll pop a cockroach in your drink and a drawing pin
>   in your shoe,
> move all the pieces on the board and ruin every game.

Azita's poetry has been translated into many languages, including Swedish, German, Dutch and French. In our choice of poems for this selection, we wanted to reflect the diversity of styles and themes in Azita's work. Her poetry is complex: individual words can have multiple meanings and paradox can inflect the logic of her poems. In these translations we have tried to remain loyal both to the rich imagery of Persian poetry, as well as help an English-speaking audience grasp the layers of meanings behind Azita's words.

ELHUM SHAKERIFAR

باران های اول اردیبهشت

بهتر است مشغول خود باشید
یا شاغل به آنچه معافتان کند   از کار دشوار عاشقی
حرفه‌ای که آدم را وا می‌دارد   تونل‌هایی بلند و کور
پشت جمله‌های کوتاه حفر کند
با چشم لک‌لک دنیا را ببیند
زبان مارمولک‌ها را یاد بگیرد
یا مورچه‌ای گیج باشد   که دانه‌های درشت را
از دیوار صاف بالا می‌برد
و از این همه مواجبش تنها
بادهای آخر پاییز باشد و
باران‌های اول اردیبهشت

THE FIRST RAINS OF SPRING

It is better to bustle away,
to be busy with some work or other
and keep love at bay.
For when it takes hold
we find significance everywhere we look,
the pelican's point of view seems persuasive,
we long to learn the language of lizards,
even an ant's dizzying ascent looks meaningful.
And what have we gained from it?
Only the last winds of autumn,
the first rains of spring.

با گلی سرخ

با گلی سرخ
از میان پیراهن‌های سیاه
و پرچم های ژنده‌ی پیاده‌رو بگذر
راهی دیگر نیست
با گل سرخت
از گوشه‌ی چپ کاغذ
پایین بیا
از لابلای خط‌ها و سطرها
عبور کن
و سمت خاطراتم بپیچ
مرا ملاقات کن
در خانه‌ای زرد و فرسوده
که لولاهای زنگ زده دارد
و دریچه‌های پوشیده از پیچک و علف
نجواهای درهم و کشدار، غبار اشیااند
لفاف غمناک سالیان
برگرد ترس ها
با گل سرخت
بیا، بیا
و چنانکه نبینند
سوی در بهشت
اشارت کن.

WITH A RED FLOWER

Wearing a poppy
leave behind those black clothes,
the flags of mourning,
the tired, disconsolate streets.
This is the only way onwards.
Wearing your red flower
climb from between these handwritten lines,
turn from the empty space of this paper
and step into my memories.

Come! Meet me
in that shabby old house,
where now the pipes are rusty,
the shutters lost in ivy and long grass,
where cobwebs and whispers have
settled over everything,
where, after all these years,
sorrow is the only dustsheet.

Come back to me, hide your fears,
wearing your red flower, come back,
but take care that no one sees
the route that brought you here from Heaven.

آب سیاه

شقایق‌ها اول آمدند و
ملخ ها
بعد وقت باد
این تمام کودکی ی چشم‌های تو بود
پیش از آب سیاه و تیغ
رشته‌های هزار مسجد
از گل‌های دیوانه رد می‌شد

اول شقایق‌ها رفته‌اند
بعد مادربزرگ و
اتاق نمور شازده
عکس اوپنهایمر و پاتریس لومومبا
مبل قرمز در حراجی‌ی الیاس

چارقدهای بته‌دار آبی رد شدند
آکاردئون و پرچم‌های عزا
ترک ها   کردها
عموهایم   با عکس‌شان   ته قلیان
مادرم در صف اول نماز جمعه   پشتش به من
برادرم عضو بسیج

GLAUCOMA

The corn poppies came first,
then the locusts
and after that the unravelling wind.
That was how childhood looked to you
before the dark water, before the thorns,
before the mountain range of a thousand mosques
cast shadow over those wild flowers .

First the poppies went
then grandmother,
then the royal rooms grew shabby,
the photos of Oppenheimer, Lumumba,
the red furniture — everything went to the second-hand shop.

Joyous accordions and flags of mourning,
Turks and Kurds,
little blue-patterned headscarves —
all passed us by in the street.
'By Appointment to…' the Princes, my mother's brothers,
was stamped on every cup and *shisha*,
my mother, first in line for Friday Prayers, kept her back to me,
my brother joined the *Bassij*.

اول ملخ‌ها می‌آیند و بعد شقایق‌ها
نه
اول شقایق‌ها رفته بودند
و ملخ‌ها...

گودی چشم   از برف پر می‌شد
دره‌های زمستان سفید است

بعد تیغ و آب‌های سیاه...

First the locusts come, then the poppies
no
first the poppies went
then the locusts…

The hollow of the eye   fills with snow,
the valleys of winter are white,
then come the thorns and the dark waters…..

نامه

سکوت خواب‌های زیادی دید
و به یاد آورد   خم شانه کسی را در آسمان
و تو پرنده‌ای شدی   با زخمی بزرگ‌تر از سایه‌ات
به یاد آورد   انگشت‌هایت را با آن رد کبود
و بال‌های بریده کوچک در پاکتی
و به یاد آورد
چقدر ما خوب جنگیده‌ایم
تا فراموشی مرگ را بغل کند
سکوت
مثل درخت ایستاده‌ای
سبز می‌شود برگ می‌دهد
و میوه‌ها ؛ فانوس روشنی از خون
طولانی‌تر از
کلماتی که ما را کوتاه‌تر برید و خالی نوشت
در این تهی
تیز است چاقوی تو
مثل گودال کنده در طول سال‌ها
پر از سیاه
سکوت ما را ادامه داد
ادا کرد ما را در خواب‌های بد
در این هوای گرفته و ابری پیچید دور ما
و آینه‌ی جیبی میان بری نداشت
تا باور کنی
باران از ابرهای تو روشن‌تر است

LETTER

In the silence dreams came
and brought to mind   your silhouette against the sky
and you   changed into a bird   carrying hurt bigger than your
    own shadow
and this brought to mind   your cold, stained fingers,
those cut and folded wings placed in an envelope
and that brought to mind
how well we fought
to the bitter end.
Silence
in which you stand like a tree
putting out green, unfolding leaves,
bountiful; a lantern glimmering with blood-red fruit
so much riper than
the sharp words that cut us short, hollowed us out.
In this emptiness
your knife is still sharp
it has gouged a pit in the passage of years
full of darkness.
Silence, in which we carried on,
making us act out bad dreams,
enfolding us in all those dark clouds,
proffering no handy little mirror for you to look in
and understand
that rain is brighter than anything your clouds had to offer.

قایقی که مرا آورد

پشت صورتی که شکل تو را دارد
اسم های قدیمی غیب می شود
خون عکس مچاله دارد
و باد پرنده‌ی مسی
انگار بیابان مرا از روی ژاکتم پوشیده باشد

برهنه نیستم
گاهی کلمات در سرفه هایم
و ماه کف آلود در لیوان گم می شود
این سفر همیشه دور زبانم چرخید
و رگ هایم از مرگ چیزی پنهان نکرد
برای کشیدن قدم هایی به خط ثلث
تابستان مرا اقرار کرده بود
این کرک سبز مچاله بر انگشت های یخ
موج به طرز زیبایی شبیه عشق می آمد
و پس می نشست

دلم برای قایقی که مرا آورد
گاهی تنگ می شود
و اینجا شاهدم برابر پلک های زمستان
همین آسمان کهنه است
و چمدانی که نیمرخ آبی ی مرا پنهان می کند.

THE BOAT THAT BROUGHT ME

Behind these eyes that look like mine
old names are fading away,
the past lies crumpled in my clenched fist —
a coppery bird in coppery wind,
this vast place has covered me from head to toe.

I am not stripped of word and thought
but sometimes what I want to say gets lost
like a moon smudged with cloud, or when I splutter on a drink.
My tongue trips up when I speak of that journey
though the blood in my veins felt the truth of death.
As I traced my footsteps through the tracery of my old language
Summer whispered to me
and my frozen fingers began to put out shoots
even as I began to love the cold ebb and flow of tides.

Sometimes I miss
the boat that brought me here,
now that I am witness to the icy eyes of a Swedish winter,
under these tired old clouds,
while that suitcase still holds a patch of the sky-blue me.

زمستان که بیاید

زمستان بیاید
شکل خودم می شوم
کتاب های دورت آتش گرفته اند
یاسمن در خواب ها   آهو می دود
سر به کوه می زند
کوه را به سادگی بغل می‌کنم
در سینه   جا می شود

دیدی ترسی نداشت
قواره ی سنگ ها

از افتادن   بالا   که می رویم
دریا   اهلی تر می آید
قلاده اش را گرفته ام

پس   مرا با کلمات نزن
شکنجه نده
تنت را به صخره نکش
تا شکل پلک‌های خونی   بمیرم

زمستان   کوچه ای صاف
انتهای همین خیابان که   بپیچی
و سال ها
همین اسب سیاه رم کرده‌اند
با انگشتت که بشمری

WHEN WINTER COMES

When winter comes
I will look in the mirror and know myself again.
On fire with ideas, my books were burning.
My daughter came to me in dreams, a deer running,
a deer that had me flee to the mountains.
Well, I can hug those mountains,
see how they nestle in my arms?

There was nothing to be afraid of after all.
The scale of these things is just a matter of perspective,
and even when we fall, we rise up again,
the sea looks calmer,
the fluffy white dog is back on its lead.

So don't berate me,
don't blame me,
don't beat me up about it,
don't make me weep blood.
Count the passing years on your fingers,
they are galloping by like a wild, dark horse
and the only thing at the end of that path is winter.

زمستان که بیاید
از هر دو سو رفته‌ایم
یکی مرا گم می کند

با آن یکی پیدا می شوم
اما باید نمی ترسیدی
و می گفتی
چرا به سینه ات چاقو فرو کرده ای
تا آدم ها در آینه فراری شوند .

When winter comes
we can go in one of two directions,
we can get lost
or we can find ourselves again.
I shouldn't have been frightened,
I should have said, *why torture yourself?*
So that those shadows melt away leaving just me in the mirror again.

برف

پهنای این ملافه از چین تا ماچین
و   بر تمام آن برف   باریده
چرا نمی‌رسیم
جز لنگه گوشواره‌ای
بر این سپیدی ردی نیست
نه درختی هست نه خرگوشی ، ستاره‌ای
کجاییم
گوشواره را که انداختي در کشو
ملافه ها را در سبد
و تاریکي را تکاندي از ایوان
مرده ام کمی کنار دست‌هایت
در انتهاي شبي که آمده بودم

بوي جنگل مي آمد
اما تمام راهها را پوشانده بود
برفي که مي بارید
مي بارد، مي پوشاند هنوز...

SNOW

This sheet that stretches from here to the world's end
 is covered by all that fallen snow.
Why must we be lost too?
Just a single stray earring
shows midst all this whiteness,
not a tree, not a rabbit, not a star.
Where are we amongst it all?

When you chucked the earring in that drawer
shook out the darkness on the balcony
and threw the sheets into the laundry basket,
at the end of that long night
I died a little.

It was a fresh, wild garden,
but every path was covered
with sheets of snow.
It is falling now, shrouding everything still …

اما

پشت به یکدیگر ایستاده‌ایم
به تماشای تاریکی و جرجر باران
باران می‌ایستد
فصلی دیگر می‌آید
سر می‌چرخانیم تا بهار را تماشا کنیم
اما یکدیگر را باز نمی‌شناسیم

BUT

We stand back to back
to contemplate darkness
and the chirping of rain,
the rain eases
a new season dawns
we turn our heads
to contemplate Spring
but find we no longer know one another.

Happy Valentine

هفت کوه شش دریا و دو آسمان تبانی کرده‌اند. دروغ‌گویند
کی به تو گفت دوستت دارم؟
توی گل‌های شیپوری زار می‌زنم از تو بیزارم
توی رودخانه‌هایت آهک می‌ریزم   روی ملافه‌ها مرکب
شکل عفریت می‌کشم روی بالش   شاخ می‌گذارم روی عکس   از تو بترسند ماهی‌ها
به دکمه‌هایم قفل می‌زنم   به نوک پستان‌هایم طلسم
همه درخت‌های کوچه‌ات را اره می‌کنم   فایل‌هایت را پاک
اسمت را چپه صدا می‌زنم   پیراهنت را می‌دزدم
قیر می‌مالم به شیشه ماشینت   میخ می‌ریزم پیچ جاده‌ها
در توالت را از رویت می‌بندم   می‌روم سینما بی‌خیال
توی لیوان سوسک می‌اندازم   توی کفش‌هایت پونز
بازی را به هم می‌زنم هر روز   مهره‌ها را از نو دوباره می‌چینم
وسط حرف‌ها یک باغوحش دریایی می‌گذارم   پشت جدایی یک فرودگاه صحرایی
شب صدای جن می‌شوم توی گوش‌هات   بمب ساعتی توی رگ و پی‌ات
کراوات میهمانی‌ات را قیچی می‌زنم زیگزاگ
حرف‌هایم را عوض می‌کنم مثل باد   کارهایت را بایگانی می‌کنم توی پوشه
صدایت اه اه؛ شبیه بوق قطار دلم را هُرری
چشم‌هایت بدتر؛ دو پیاله مسی؛ پر از قند و حلوا
تو بدجور بوی زعفران و گل سرخ می‌دهی
قلبت پر از ماهی قرمز وول وول توی هم
بعد از این هرچه بپرسی راست می‌گویم   هرچه بگویی انکار
توی موهایت کوکتل مولوتوف پرت می‌کنم   رمبو شوی
انگشتم فرو توی رویاها   چک چک کند حالت
دستکاری می‌کنم خوابت را   قورباغه‌ها سوزن می‌شوند زیر لحاف
پرنده‌های شعر را اسب می‌کشم بالای درخت   زن‌ها قوری چینی روی میز اتاق
سنجاب و شیر و مورچه‌خوار قاطی هم   می‌شود توعینا
گربه زخم و زگیل بلا را نمی‌شود ول کرد توی لوله بخاری
ستاره نچسباند جز زززززز رو بپیشانی اش   وقتی گم می‌شود
تمام فلش‌های دنیا خمیده‌اند   سمت دندان‌های تو
کوچه‌ها تا خورده‌اند پله پله   تا فرق سرم
گیج درگیر حفظ شماره طولانی توام   بی‌برج و قلعه روزهای دنیا فرعی‌اند
در استخدام تماشا این گوش و چشم‌های قیقاج خسته از اضافه‌کاری مدام
از تق و توق چکش‌هایم روی دیوارت   بشقاب‌ها زاییده‌اند

HAPPY VALENTINE

They say it was like the collision of seven mountains, six oceans and two
     hemispheres. Well, they lied.
Who told you I love you? I lament to the lilies, *Actually, I hate you!*
I will fill your rivers with limes, flood your sheets with ink,
I'll draw the devil on your pillow and scare the fish with the horns
     and tail I pin on you.
I'll make my nipples irresistible and put padlocks on my blouse.
I will cut down every tree on your street and delete your every file,
I will call your name out backwards, I will steal your shirt,
I'll smear tar on your windscreen, scatter nails at the bend in the road,
I'll lock you in the loo and go see a film without a backward glance,
I'll pop a cockroach in your drink and a drawing pin in your shoe,
move all the pieces on the board and ruin every game,
I'll put a desert between us, a whole teeming ocean.
I'll cut your fancy tie into zigzags, I'll slip explosives into your nervous
     system. Each night I'll fill your ears with wailing banshees.
I'll let myself change my mind at the drop of a hat but of your every move
     I'll keep a log.
The very sound of you — Oh god! — it sets my teeth on edge — and,
     even worse,
your gloopy eyes, like bowls of syrup, your stink of saffron and red roses,
your heart full of goodluck goldfish, wriggling up against each other!
You know what? If you want to ask me something, I'll tell you straight —
     but if you accuse me of anything, I'll just deny it!
I'll pour a Molotov cocktail into your hair; so you'll look like that picture
     of Rimbaud,
I'll stick my fingers into your dreams, to mess you up altogether,
I'll take over your sleep; you'll think there are frogs needling you under
     those sheets.
I'll turn the sweetest most tender images into ugly ones;
instead of beautiful birds I'll draw horses in the treetops. You know those
     big fat women on Russian dolls? I'll graffiti them all over your table!

دوری از چنگال‌های تیزم   رجز می‌خوانند سازهای نق‌نقو توی دلم
سماع می‌کنند فیل‌ها روی حلقه آتش
می‌رقصند روی بشکه   خرس‌های دامن گلی
زنجیری هندوستان شدم   از لهجه‌ی طوطی‌های دیوانه‌ات
کاش قفس بیاورند اژدها ادب شود   اردیبهشت را دوباره بچینند برای بَبر
تا شیپوری‌های سفید را نخورده این میمون حریص
دنیا را نریخته نپاشیده روی دامنش هیولا
عشق همین گل سرخی است که می‌بندم به سنگ من و پرتاب می‌کنم سمت شیشه‌هایت ناغافل
جرنگ و جرینگ و جرنگ
گرمب

I'll make you look like a squirrel crossed with a lion and anteater.
Yet I can't just dump you — a tatty, tormenting Tomcat
that can't even find his own way home.
Every arrow points to you. This accordion of streets folds back to you.
But I'm dizzy trying to climb all these summits and towers, trying to
    learn by heart your long number; these ears and eyes of mine are
    worn out with it.
I've banged on your walls so hard the plates are smashed to smithereens.
You may be far away from my sharp barbs but deep inside me it's as if
    elephants sing, spinning hoops of fire and flowery-skirted bears
    dance on barrels.
Your mad jabbering parrots have even got me hooked on an idea of India.
If only there was some way to tame this dragon, to put the tiger back in
    its cage. If only it could be Spring again,
before this greedy animal eats up all the white lilies,
before this monster completely destroys her entire world.
Love is like a red rose that I tie to the stone of myself and aim at your
    window.
Tinkle, tinkle, tinkle.
Crash!